A Chance to Grow

Shlesma Parajuli

BookLeaf
Publishing

Presentation by *BookLeaf Publishing*

Web: www.bookleafpub.com

E-mail: info@bookleafpub.com

ISBN: 9789395620246

First edition 2022

DEDICATION

This collection is dedicated to all those little girls who ever in their life had a little doubt about themselves and their abilities. We all go through some kind of self-doubt at some point in our lives. We just have to aim that someday we will be independent and be able to love ourselves unconditionally.

Little Girl

Little girl in a new world
Keeping big dreams in her eyes
Fear of the unknown
New world around her
Can she overcome
All the hardships that come her way?

Grew up in a new place
All the knowledge at her fingertips
Knew she needed to believe in herself
And one day her dreams will be fulfilled.

Be careful little girl
Look inside your heart
Focus on the light
Imagine your life
Surrounded by love and loved ones
Love yourself little girl
The greatest strength a person can have.

Waiting

Been waiting for the time to be myself
But sometimes it is hard to be
Always worried about other people's feelings
Which makes me want to keep on waiting.

It is hard to put myself out there
Knowing I have so much to fear
Sometimes I wonder what will it take
To be completely free from all the mistakes

Want to be true to myself without fearing
Confusion etched in my mind
Cannot decide right from wrong
Cannot shake this feeling that I might just be
waiting.

Time

Time heals all wounds
That's all we hear every time
but one of the best things in life
Is when a person works towards healing
themselves.

We have all the time in the world
When used to our own advantage
Instead, we spend our life
Wondering what if's for things unnecessary.

Things in life change over time
One day we are the happiest
Then there are some days when we feel low
Every circumstance changes us for the better.

Over time we all realize things
It makes us a better person
Learning from things in the past
That's one way to be satisfied in life.

I Feel

I feel good
Like being cleansed by the rain.

I feel like myself
Finally being able to accept.

I feel positive energy from within
The power to stand up for me

I feel loved and supported
The unconditional feeling

I feel like I can love myself wholeheartedly
Without any reservations.

I feel like the clouds are parting
Bringing with it clear skies and happiness.

Feelings

I have lived with this for so long
The feeling of doubt
Have tried to let it go
Nothing seems to be working at all.

The more I dwell
The more I think
It is not like I do not want to come out of it
It is purely because I do not know how to.

Days turn into weeks
Weeks turn into months
Believing still feels impossible
Whether in myself or on others.

Want to conquer this feeling
Instead of it dragging me down
The reward seems impossible to reach
Risking everything is the only way I see it.

What will it take?

What will it take?
To overcome this fear
This sensation of dread and emptiness
Dazed and confused by the world around me
Will I prosper?
Or will I fall more in the quicksand?

What will it take?
To be okay with myself
The feeling of never being enough
And not knowing what to do next.

What will it take?
To see myself in a different light
When there are no doubts
Looking in the mirror.

What will it take?
To be completely happy
Feeling lighter than ever
No weights on my shoulder.

Sunrise to Sunset

Sunrise
It's a beautiful sight
But why do I feel so hollow inside
Bursting with people everywhere
And I am still here alone anyway.

Mind wandering around and around
Like hopping from one step to the next
Doesn't seem to settle at all
this feeling of restlessness inside.

Day passes by
But the feeling is the same
Drowned out by
All the noises around.

Sun is setting past the cityscape
Bringing with it the night all around
Sparkling lights are everywhere
Filled my heart with calmness.

Feel as though I was wrong again
As I look toward my group of friends
They look over and smile at me
And something settles within me.

Is it?

Is it okay?
To not feel happy all the time
When nothing is going our way
And all you want to do is
Run away to a new place.

Is it enough?
Doing our best, but not as expected
People say what they want
They only see and judge the outcome
They don't see the process to the destination.

Is it fine?
To listen to the inner voice
That tells us what we need to hear
Tests our boundaries in troubled times
When we fall to the bottom to come out on top.

Is it happiness?
When you feel light
The darkness is fading away
Taking with it the feeling of dread
And we can see the light at the end of the tunnel.

All I ask

All I ask is
Appreciate the little things I do
Love me the way I love you
Give me the respect that I'm allowed
Do the little things the same way I do.

All I ask is
Know that I am doing my best
Have some faith in me
Give me time when I ask you to
Protect me as I protect you.

All I ask is
Recognize me in spite of my blemishes
Encourage me to look in the mirror
Look at myself
To the pure and innocent soul.

All I ask is
Believe in my abilities
Believe in my place in this world
Believe that not everything is hard
Believe in me.

She's

She's looking for inspiration
She's waiting for the right moment
She wants some motivation
She just wants love and support.

She's looking for an outlet
She wants to relieve her heart
She has many thoughts running around her head
She's just looking to unburden herself.

She's looking to find herself
In a world that's confusing
She's hoping to come out of her shell
All she wants is a little time and space.

Me

Taking care of other people
And neglecting myself
Worrying constantly
Is that all there is?
One or the other

When will I feel like a priority
When will I see the light
I don't want to say never
But if that is the case
Never cannot come fast enough.

Finally

Days turn into weeks
Weeks turn into months
Months turn into years
Believing still feels impossible
Whether in myself or on others.

Wishing to dream of a world
Where everyone's dreams come true
Where there is no limit
Where anyone can be anything
A world where I can be happy.

Clarity in mind
Helps our soul
A void in our hearts
Disrupts out happiness

Finally the clouds part
The sky is clear and blue
The emptiness is gone
And the horizon can be seen.

Healing

Uncertain times
Uncertain thoughts
Feeling like you don't belong anywhere
Beginning of self-doubt
Where did the happiness go?
Am I too broken to fix?
Am I too messed up to start healing?

Time ticks by
Have no idea where to start
Feeling dizzy all of a sudden
Negative thoughts plaguing my mind
When will I start living again?
How am I supposed to believe in myself?
When will I start healing?

Love and support
Everyone needs
Surviving in this world
Alone, cannot be done
Will I finally start to smile?
Can I move past the hurt and doubt?

For the first time, In a long time
I don't feel the dread

When I wake up, I welcome the day
I feel fine, I say
To anyone who wants to listen
Finally, there is positivity in my life.

Everyday

Every day felt like a struggle
Why was I just going through the motions?
Why couldn't I just move forward?
Would it have been too much to ask?

Wanted everything to settle
And for me to start enjoying life
Why couldn't I just let it be?
Why did it feel tough?
Like a heavy weight was on my shoulders.

Eventually, the wish came true
The storm passed
And the sun was shining
I could smell the trees and flowers
The freedom of exploring
The joy of life
And finally, I was happy again.

Remember

Remember those words
The ones who hurt you
The ones that made you doubt your worth
Forget them.

Remember those looks you used to get
The self-consciousness
Feeling your skin crawling
Come out of it.

Remember the gossip
The rumors that spread
None of them being true
Do not think about them.

Remember you control your future
The people in the past
They can talk all they want
You will come out of it stronger.

Remember you are surrounded
By people who love you
You support system
Without a doubt in their mind.

What If

We go through life
Wondering many things
And sometimes we think of
Different scenarios.

'What if' is the most common
The thought that hounds us
We are powerless against it
Because it's constantly there.

When we're younger
The thoughts are innocent
It grows with us
Not needing any permission

When we are older
The thoughts are more specific
It is directly dependent
On what we're feeling

We have to move away
From misleading thoughts
Those are the most
Hard to get rid of

'What if' is just a simple thought
If we do not give it power
In our minds and our thoughts
And finally, overcome it.

Can I

Why is it so easy?
For me to say sorry
Without it being
Ever my fault.

Why can't I let it go?
The feeling of uncertainty
Always reminding me
Of the worst expectations.

Can I ever come out of it
Will I be able to one day
Not say sorry
Not Apologize

Can I live my life
Without any doubts
Reeling me back to the present
And changing my ways.

Overcome

We are capable
We can do it
It is the thought that counts
To go past the start line.

Slowly but surely
We start living
Treating ourselves better
And overcoming the bad thoughts.

Positive thoughts are all that matter
About the world and ourselves
Once we start to smile
The sun will shine on our side.

Overcoming things is not so easy
But it can be done
Once we put our minds to it
Nothing is impossible.

Real or Fake

What can we do
When life throws stuff at us
Do we just accept it
Or fight for what we believe.

Friends are supposed to be there
Every step of our life
But what do we expect them to do
Be with you having your back

What if they do not want to
Because the reality is always there
It is hard to find real or fake
Whether they are jewelry or friends.

Real friends are like diamonds
Hard to find but special
They have your back in everything
And don't regret anything.

You are nothing without friends
Because they are your shadow
Whatever you do, they reflect
Like a transparent river.

So we got to be wise
Because life is full of surprises
People, things, and ourselves
Makes us who we are and who we will be.

Journey

Journey of a lifetime
All you need is a belief
In the people you surround yourself by
In every small aspect of your life.

Journey to find yourself
To feel happy from within
Without the confusion as to how
When nothing goes our way.

Journey to love yourself
By evolving individually
Being calm and collected
And finding the strength.

Journey to love others
No matter what the situation is
The force that binds us to them
And makes us feel loved.

Life

Life changes a lot
From good to bad in a split second.

Life is full of mysteries
Don't know what is going to happen next.

Life keeps giving us surprises
With things that we don't expect.

Life is nothing without happiness
The feeling of being on the top.

Life has its own way
Of telling us who we are.

Life is full of weird people
But we cannot live without them after all.

Life is positively complete
With a friend who is meant to be.

Life has all we love
We just need to appreciate it.